FOREX

Trading Strategies & Analysis for Beginners
Learn Market Strategy Basics with this Fundamental Guide

Descrierea CIP a Bibliotecii Naţionale a României
CARTER, MATTHEW G.
    Forex : trading strategies & analysis for beginners learn
market strategy basics with this fundamental guide / by
Matthew G. Carter. - Bucureşti : My Ebook, 2018
    ISBN 978-606-983-607-1

339

FOREX

TRADING STRATEGIES & ANALYSIS FOR
BEGINNERS. LEARN MARKET STRATEGY
BASICS WITH THIS FUNDAMENTAL GUIDE

My Ebook Publishing House
Bucharest, 2018

CONTENTS

INTRODUCTION

I want to thank you and congratulate you for buying the book, *"Forex: Trading Strategies & Analysis for Beginners; Learn Market Strategy Basics with this Fundamental Guide"*.

This book contains proven steps and strategies on how you can start trading in the foreign exchange market.

Successful Forex traders are now earning incredible amounts of money every day thanks to the high liquidity of the Forex market. However, there are also stories about people losing a lot of money in a single day. It takes knowledge, skills, and discipline in following the right strategies before you can become successful in this platform.

Written as practical guide for people who want to get a jumpstart in the Forex market world, this ebook can help you learn:

•The basic concepts behind the foreign exchange market

•The basic skills you have to learn to become successful in forex trading

•The top strategies, tips, and tricks that successful forex traders are using

•The common mistakes that you should avoid to prevent losing your capital down the drain

Thanks again for purchasing this book, I hope you enjoy it!

of this publication is strictly prohibited and any storage of this document is not allowed unless with written permission from the publisher. All rights reserved.

The information provided herein is stated to be truthful and consistent, in that any liability, in terms of inattention or otherwise, by any usage or abuse of any policies, processes, or directions contained within is the solitary and utter responsibility of the recipient reader. Under no circumstances will any legal responsibility or blame be held against the publisher for any reparation, damages, or monetary loss due to the information herein, either directly or indirectly.

Respective authors own all copyrights not held by the publisher.

The information herein is offered for informational purposes solely, and is universal as so. The presentation of the information is without contract or any type of guarantee assurance.

The trademarks that are used are without any consent, and the publication of the trademark is without permission or backing by the trademark owner. All trademarks and brands within this book are for clarifying purposes only and are the owned by the owners themselves, not affiliated with this document.

Chapter 1 - Forex Market 101

The forex market refers to the foreign exchange market that is considered as the most exciting and busiest financial market today. Decades ago, this market was only accessible to financial firms, large companies, millionaires, hedge funds, and central banks. But with technological advances such as electronic banking and the rise of the Internet, anyone can now trade in the forex market.

The fluctuations in the foreign exchange market every day are usually very small. Hundreds of currency pairs are fluctuating less than one per cent daily and that only represent less than one per cent movement in the currency value. Therefore, it is safe to say that this market has less volatility compared to the equities market. Many speculators in the forex market are depending on the availability of large leverage to increase the value of potential fluctuations.

In the retail forex, the leverage can be as high as 250:1, which is regarded as high liquidity but high risk. Moreover, 24/7 trading enables forex brokers to standardize significant leverage to make the movements more lucrative for traders.

The accessibility of high leverage as well as extreme liquidity have driven the evolution of the foreign exchange market and become a viable trading platform even for small traders. It is now possible to trade positions within a few minutes. The price fluctuations in the forex market depend on the objective evaluation of the demand and supply of the currency pair, and could be really difficult to control because of the market size. Even central banks don't have the power to influence currency prices.

The forex market can become a profitable ground for investors and traders. However, this can only be possible if you really understand the basic concepts that influence the forex market.

My goal in writing this eBook is to help you develop a basic understanding of the forex market before you even start trading in the forex market. In this book, you will also learn the most basic forex trading strategies that are commonly used by successful FX traders. Remember, don't begin trading without understanding how the market works first, unless you want to learn in the process and risk losing a substantial amount of money.

Introduction to the Forex Market

The foreign exchange market refers to the actual market where market participants can trade or speculate currencies. It plays an important role in the global economy, because the currencies must be converted first before anyone can facilitate business. For instance, if you are located in Singapore, and you want to buy 500 sacks of curry powder from India, you must pay the Indian supplier in Rupees (INR). This means that you should exchange the equal value of the Singaporean Dollars (SGD) into INR.

Foreign exchange market is also important for travel and tourism. A French tourist cannot pay in Francs to visit the Great Wall of China, because Francs is not the accepted currency in the country. Therefore, you must exchange Francs to Yuan at the current price.

The need to exchange currencies for business and personal purposes influences the high liquidity in the foreign exchange market. In terms of size, the equities market may fade in comparison. Around $5 Trillion are traded in the foreign exchange market daily.

One defining feature of this worldwide trading platform is that there is no specific organization or firm that is administering the trade. You can trade in the forex market through digital channels via over the counter or OTC transactions.

The transactions can happen online in several spots around the world rather than a single central platform. It is also available 24 hours a day and 5 days a week, and the currencies are traded worldwide in top financial centers like London, Tokyo, Frankfurt, Singapore, Sydney, New York, Zurich, Hong Kong, and Paris. This transcends across different time zones, so if the trade is already closing in Hong Kong, the platform is starting in New York.

In general, there are three options in trading in the forex market:

1. Spot market
2. Forwards market
3. Futures market

Trading in the spot market is regarded as the busiest, because this serves as the underlying platform for the forwards and the futures market. In the past, the futures market was the busiest platform for traders, because it mainly caters to private investors as well as traders in an expanded time.

But with the rise of online trading, the spot market has enjoyed a considerable flow in investments and now goes head to head with the futures market as one of the most active trading platform for individual investors and speculators. There is a high chance that your idea of the forex market is the spot market. The futures and forwards markets are usually the ideal platform for companies who need to hedge their risks to specific date in the future.

The Spot Market

In general, the spot market is the platform where you could buy and sell currencies according to the prevailing rates. The price can be affected by the present demand and supply and is also affected by various factors like currency pair performance perception, current interest rates, economic performances, and political situations (international and domestic).

The spot deal in the spot market refers to the finalized deal. This is a dual-channel transaction, in which one party will provide an agreed currency rate. The transaction is paid when the position is closed. While the spot market is known as the platform where you can deal with forex trade in the present, the trades may take around two to three days to be settled.

Forwards and Futures Markets

There is no actual trading of currencies in the forwards and futures markets. Instead, market participants are dealing with contracts that signify a claim to specific type of currency and a specific unit price. The settlement is specified at a future date.

In the futures market, the contracts are traded based on a standard size and the settlement date for public financial markets such as the Mercantile Exchange in Chicago. In the US, the futures market is governed by the National Futures Association. These contracts have specific details including the units for trading, data settlement, and the price increases. The exchange serves as a representative of the trader for clearing and settlement of the contract.

In the forwards market, the contracts are traded over the counter between two players who will specify the terms based on their agreements. International companies are mainly trading contracts in these markets to hedge against fluctuations in the exchange rate. Forex speculators are also participating in these trading platforms.

Brief History of the Forex Market

With the worldwide scale of the forex market, you need first to understand important historical events, which are related to the currency system we use today as well as how the forex market has evolved over time before you try trading or investing.

The Gold Standard

The Gold Standard model was established in 1875 as a global currency model. This became one of the early milestones of the forex market. Prior to this standard, countries in the 19th century usually use precious metals like gold or silver for international payments. The main disadvantage of this system was the volatility of gold and silver prices as it is influenced by the supply and demand. For example, depletion of primary gold reserves in a specific country can have lasting effects on the prices of gold.

In the gold standard, governments or companies have to agree to convert their currencies into specific equivalent of gold and vice versa. Hence, the currency should be backed by actual gold in reserve. And so, the governments during the 19th century have to secure sufficient gold reserves to catch up with the demand for exchanging foreign currencies.

Leading world economies at that time such as Great Britain and China have already established the value of currency. Eventually, the distinction in the price of gold between two currencies was regarded as the rate of exchange between the two currencies. This became the early standard for trading currencies.

But on the onset of World War I, the gold standard eventually became obsolete. Because of imminent danger from the Axis Power, many European countries had to finance massive military projects. Gold reserves were not enough as they need to complete the project within a limited timeframe.

After the war, some countries re-established the gold standard, but most economies discarded the system again when war erupts again in the 1940s. However, gold continues to be valued as the preferred channel for international payments.

The United States Dollar Standard

Before the end of World War II, the Allied Forces deemed it crucial to establish a currency system to solve the downsides of the gold standard. So in 1944, a meeting was convened at the Bretton Woods, NH to deliberate on a new currency management system. The resulting system was later on called the Bretton Woods System.

The Allied Forces agree to adhere to the following:

•Use a fixed rate system for trading currencies

•Use United States Dollars as the primary reserve currency to replace gold

•Form three worldwide agencies to manage economic activities: the International Monetary Fund (IMF), the World Bank, and the General Agreement on Tarrif and Trade (GATT).

Bretton Woods became the birthplace of the US Dollar as a global reserve currency. Furthermore, USD was also established to be the only currency to have an actual equivalent of gold reserves.

As such, the US had to execute a series of balancing the deficit payments to make sure that the currency is the most stable in the world. However, in the 1970s, the US gold reserves were not sufficient to sustain the economic activities of the world.

In 1971, US Pres. Richard Nixon ended the Bretton Woods System by officially declaring the termination of the gold reserve system for the USD. In spite of the fact that the Bretton Woods system was a short-lived system, it still made an important contribution to the present-day world economy.

When the Bretton Woods disintegrated, world governments gradually embraced the floating rates for foreign exchange. But in 1976, the Jamaica Agreement led to the permanent elimination of the gold reserve standard. However, this doesn't mean that government totally adopted the floating rate system. Many governments are still using floating rates, pegged rates, or dollar rates.

Floating Rates Mechanism

This exchange mechanism is established if the exchange rate of a currency is permitted to freely change in value according to the market forces of demand and supply. However, the central bank or the state could still interfere to ensure the stability of the currency if the exchange rates experience high fluctuation.

For instance, if the currency of a country is falling too much, the government may choose to increase short-term interest rates. This will in turn cause the currency to slightly appreciate. But take note that this is a very basic explanation as central banks usually employ several tools for currency management.

Pegged Rates

Pegging refers to the practice of a country establishing a fixed exchange rate for another currency so that it becomes more stable compared to regular floating rates.

In particular, pegging will allow the currency of a country to have a fixed rate for the exchange with one or a specified group of foreign currencies. In addition, the currency may only fluctuate if there is a change in the pegged currencies.

In 1997 and 2005, the Chinese government pegged its currency to the US dollar at USD 1 to CNY 8.28. The disadvantage of pegging is that the value of the currency is now on the discretion of the economy of the country. For instance, when USD significantly increases its value against other denominations, the value of the Chinese Yuan will also increase.

Dollarization

Dollarization happens if a country decides not to use its own currency and adopts the United States Dollars as its currency. Even though dollarization normally bestows a country with higher stability, the disadvantage is that the central bank of the country cannot make any form of monetary policy or print its own money. Countries that adopted the US dollars include Zimbabwe, British Virgin Islands, Palau, Marshall Islands, El Salvador, East Timor, and Ecuador.

Reading Currency Quote

When you are quoting a currency, you are doing it in relation to the currency of another country in a way that the value is defined by the other currency's value. Hence, if you are want to know the forex rate between the Swiss Francs (CHF) and Chinese Yuan (CNY), the forex quotation will look like this:

CHF/CNY = 6.95

This is known as the currency pair. In this pair, CHF is the currency base, while CNY is the counter currency. The former always has a value of one unit, and the latter is what that one base unit is equivalent in its denomination. This FX pair means that CHF1 = 6.95 Chinese Yuan. So if you have one Swiss Franc, you can buy 6.95 Chinese Yuan. Take note that the FX quote includes the currency symbol for the currency pairs.

You can quote a currency pair either indirectly or directly. A quote is referred to as indirect when the local currency is the currency base, while a direct quote is basically a forex pair wherein the domestic currency is the quote currency.

Therefore, if you are looking for the United States Dollar as the domestic currency and the Japanese Yen as the foreign currency, an indirect code will be JPY/USD, while a direct quote will be USD/JPY

In a direct quotation, the quote currency could vary, while the currency base has a default value of one unit. Meanwhile, in the indirect quote, the domestic currency has a default value of one unit, while the foreign currency has a variable value.

For instance, if the Japanese Yen is the domestic unit, a direct quote will be 109.37 USD/JPY, which means that 1 unit of USD can buy JPY 109.37. The indirect for this will be inverse (1/109.37), 0.0091 JPY/USD, which means with 1 JPY, you can buy USD 0.0091.

In the FX spot market, most currencies are traded against the USD, and this is often referred to as the currency base. These are all direct quotes and true to the above CHF/CNY that indicate 1 CHF is equal to 6.95 CNY.

You must remember that not all currencies have the USD as the base. The currencies used by the British Commonwealth such as the New Zealand Dollar, Australian Dollar, and the British Pound are all identified as the currency base against the USD. This is how we also quote the Euro. For these situations, the USD is positioned as the counter currency, and the FX rate is known as indirect. Hence, EUR to USD is quoted as 1.19, because one unit of Euro can buy 1.19 USD.

The exchange currency rates are quoted up to 4 decimal digits. One exception of this is the JPY, because this currency is quoted only up to 2 decimal digits.

If a currency quote is given without the USD as a component, this is known as cross currency. The most popular cross-currencies are the EUR/CHF, EUR/JPY, and the EUR/GBP. In general, currency pairs expand the trading horizons in the FX market. But you should bear in mind that they are not that much popular compared to the currency pair that uses USD as the currency base.

Buying and Selling Price

Like in stock markets, if you are trading currency pairs, you have to refer to the buying rate (bid) and selling price (ask). Take note that these are still in relation to the currency base. If your strategy is to go long (trading on a currency pair) the asking price refers to the rate of quote currency, which should be paid so you can purchase currency base units, or how much the market is willing to sell currency base units in reference to the currency quote.

On the other hand, when you go short, the bid rate signifies the amount of currency quoted you can get when you sell currency base units or how much the market is willing to shell out for the currency (quoted) in reference to the currency base.

Remember, the figure on the left of the slash is the bid rate, while the asking price is located after the slash. Take note that it is customary that the full price's last two digits are quoted.

The bid is also smaller compared to the asking price. Take a look at an example below:

USD/CHF = 1.3000/05

Ask = 1.3005

Bid = 1.3000

Buying this FX pair signifies that you like to purchase the currency base, and so you have to refer to the asking price to know the value in Swiss Francs the trade will charge for USD. Based on our asking price, you can purchase $ 1.00 with 1.3005 Swiss Francs, which is the currency that you are quoting.

You have to refer to the bid if you want to short this FX pair or simply you want to put the currency base in the market using the quote currency. This signifies that the forex market will purchase $1 currency base for a price that is equivalent of 1.3000 Swiss Francs, which is the currency that you are quoting.

The currency base (whichever you are quoting first) always refer to the one in which we are conducting the transaction. This means, you can either buy or sell currency base. You can refer to the specific currency pair rate in order to find the price depending on what currency you like to use for selling or buying the base with.

Spreads

The difference between the ask price and the bid price is known as the spread. For example, in our currency pair: USD / JPY = 109.2418/21, the spread is 0.0021 or 3 points or pips. Even though the difference may be very small for the untrained eye, even the slightest movement could lead to thousands of profits or loses. This is one reason why speculators are always monitoring the movements in the forex market as even the smallest point change could lead to substantial profits.

Pips

Pips refer to the lowest value that a forex price could move in a forex quote. For example, for USD, EUR, GBP, and CHF, a pip is equivalent to 0.0001. And with the Japanese Yen, a pip is equal to 0.01, because as we have noted earlier in this chapter, Yen is quoted up to two decimal points only. Hence, in a forex quote, USD/EUR, the pip will be 0.0001 Euro. Many currencies could be traded inside a range of at least 100 to a max of 150 pips in a single day.

The Futures and the Forwards Markets

Bear in mind that an important differentiating factor between the forex markets is how we quote currencies. Within the forwards or futures markets, the currencies are always traded against USD. Therefore, the pricing is conducted in terms of how many USD you have to purchase a certain currency.

Take note that in the forex spot market, some currencies are traded against USD, while there are also quotes where USD is traded against them. Hence, the quotes from the futures / forwards market as well as the spot market will not usually become aligned to each other.

As an example, in the forex spot market, the Euro is quoted with the US Dollars as EUR/USD. This is also the manner used for quoting currencies in the futures and forwards market. Hence, if the Euro becomes stronger than the US dollar in the spot market, there is also a high tendency to rise in the futures and forwards markets.

Meanwhile, in the case of the USD / JPY currency pair, USD is quoted against JPY. The current quote in the spot market for this FX pair is 110.27, which means that $1 will be able to buy 110.27 Japanese Yen. But in the futures FX market, the quote will be .0090 or (1/110.27), which means that 1 Japanese Yen will purchase .0090 US Dollar.

Hence, a slight increase in the USD/JPY in the spot market will result to a fall in the yen futures rate since USD will be stronger against the yen and so one unit of yen will buy fewer dollars.

Currency Cross Rates

Even though most of the currency trading includes USD, top foreign currencies can be traded among themselves. Currency cross rate refers to the currency trading pair that does not include USD. For example, a Japanese company with sales in New Zealand may wish to convert the New Zealand Dollars it has received back into Japanese Yen.

There is no need for the company to convert the payments in NZD into USD before they can convert USD into JPY. Rather, the Japanese company could use the NZD cross rate to convert the NZD directly into Yen.

As you already know, the USD and the GBP are among the most heavily traded currencies in the world. Considering that by definition, USD is not included in the currency cross rates, the most heavily traded cross-rate currency pairs include the Euro.

Cross currency rate pairs are also quite popular among other top foreign currencies such as the Swiss Franc, Chinese Yuan, and the British Pound. Other currencies that are less liquid usually don't actively trade except against USD. If you are interested in transacting between these currencies, you might need to complete two transactions. First, you have to convert the foreign currency into USD, then convert the USD into your preferred currency.

Chapter 2 - Basic Forex Trading Skills You Need to Learn

There are many ways to become a successful forex trader. For example, if you want to be a forex trader under a financial firm, they usually hire people who have strong background in hard sciences, engineering, or math. In starting your career as a forex trader, there are basic skills you need to learn. This includes the following:

1. Analytical skills
2. Research skills
3. Focus and Control
4. Money management
5. Psychology

Analytical Skills for Forex Trading

Analytical thinking is a basic skill that every forex trader should have. You must be able to analyze available data within a limited time frame. Forex trading is a numbers game and the platform is filled with patterns, indicators, and charts that you need to analyze quickly.

You also need to develop your analytical skills so you can easily identify trends in the forex market.

There are two types of analysis that you need to master with forex trading: technical and fundamental analysis.

Technical Analysis

Among the fundamental concepts of technical analysis is that the future price movement could be predicted by looking into past movements. Because the foreign exchange market is a 24-hour market, you get a chance to assess a huge volume of data, which you can use to measure the price activity, which increases the statistical significance of the projection. Many investors and traders in the forex market are using technical tools like indicators, charts, and trends.

In general, it is crucial to take note that technical analysis interpretation could stay the same regardless of the assets that you are keeping track. In this Chapter, we will discuss the most popular forex strategies based on technical analysis.

In doing technical analysis in the forex market, you need to determine if a currency pair will trend in a specific direction, or if it will remain in the range or go against the trend. A common way to figure out these traits is to place trend lines, which links historical levels that have avoided a rate from going lower or higher. These resistance and support levels are popular among technical traders to find out if the current trend shall continue.

Common Indicators in Technical Analysis

Forex traders who prefer technical analysis use various indicators alongside resistance and support levels to help them in projecting the future direction of exchange rates. Take note that learning how to understand different technical indicators is crucial and may require further study on your part.

Among the indicators that you should learn well include stochastics, moving average convergence divergence (MACD), moving averages, Fibonacci retracement, and Bollinger Bands. Take note that these tools are not often used as an independent indicator but rather alongside chart patterns and other indicators.

Fibonacci Indicator

The Fibonaccis Indicator is a common indicator used in technical analysis in the forex market. This strategy heavily depends on the pullback and to completely understand how this works, you should revisit your understanding of the forex trend. In looking at every price action separately, it is quite difficult to look for a pattern. Taking a closer look at the larger picture will allow you to identify the trends.

For hundreds of years, the Fibonacci ratios and numbers have been popular among artists and mathematicians. These figures signify many things in mathematics, in nature, and even in the financial markets. Although Fibonacci is a classic concept in mathematics, you don't need to be well adept in the subject so you can use these figures in calculating projections in the forex trading platforms. All you have to do is to make a decision according on the lines that appear on the charts.

By taking a closer look on how far the pullback has reached on the Fibonacci scale, we could figure out if the price could pull back again or turn into a bearish or bullish trend. As long as the price will remain above the specific line, you could expect the trends to pull back through a rising trend. When the price crosses the line, you should treat it as a beginning of a bearish trend that will indicate that it is time to close the position.

Horizontal Levels

Horizontal Levels are among the most simple but quite useful concepts trading in the forex market. These are fundamentals in most forex trading strategies and could help you in studying charts. But you can also use them as a separate strategy instead of a mere tool to ride along with other strategies.

In monitoring the most clear-cut price actions and identifying the horizontal levels, you can make profitable trades. In completely becoming familiar with the horizontal levels of advanced charts, you can identify trends that you might have otherwise ignored.

Swing Points

The ideal method in using horizontal levels to your advantage is through the analysis of swing points, which refer to the points where there is a change in trends. By marking the horizontal levels on these places, you can find the prices where there could be a likely change in the trend.

Ranging Markets

Horizontal levels can be used in ranging markets, which refers to the condition in which the price has clear lower and upper boundaries. By monitoring the price when it is approaching a limit, you can project with precision the points where the price could be more likely to continue in the next trend.

Divergence

Traders as well as analysts of financial markets, aside from the market fundamentals, are using several indicators to determine what could happen to the price of a specific instrument. These indicators will provide you a basic method of recognizing patterns and projecting which way the price could trend. Using these indicators is what makes signals in the forex market helpful, as you can use them for real-time analysis of the price action.

Fundamental Analysis

In the stock market, fundamental analysis measures the true value of a company. A fundamentalist (one who mainly uses fundamental analysis) bases his decision to invest or trade in stocks according to the calculation.

Somehow, this is similar in the foreign exchange market, where fundamentalists are also looking into the true value of the countries and their currencies. They are also watching out for economic announcements in order to gain an idea of the true value of the currency.

In general, geo-political events, economic data, and news reports from a certain country are regarded similarly to announcements about stocks and companies used by investors to gain insight of their true value. The value may change over time because of several factors including financial strength and growth. Fundamentalists are focusing on this data to assess the currency of the countries in the currency pair that they are interested in.

Forex Carry Trade

The forex carry trade is an investment strategy wherein a trader is offering a currency that has lower interest rates and buys a currency with higher interest rates. To put it simply, you are lending currencies at a higher rate and borrow at a lower rate. In using this strategy, you can make profits through the difference between these two rates.

Trading the News

Significant news events around the world could have a large impact on the foreign exchange market, which usually render all analysis meaningless. Take note that the forex market is a 24-hour market, and there is no way to schedule the announcement of news. Changes in the market according to the economy and data could hit any type of trader wherever you are and whichever currency you choose to trade.

Short Term News Trading

Short term news trading is a bit more challenging because of the volatility as well as the tighter stops. More often than not, minutes before and after, there are whipsaws with the rate frantically moving in both directions. Short term news trading is also divided into several strategies:

One method is to sell the currency spike after a bad news. There are instances that even after bad announcements, the price slightly increases for several seconds or even minutes. This is the best time to sell, particularly if it is at some significant resistance or level.

Long Term News Trading

In looking for long-term trading opportunities according to economic news, it is crucial to assess both the previous and current data. This is because there are instances that news may take weeks or months to be significantly absorbed by the market. You can use the information to see a larger picture and the impact that it may have on the currency you want to trade. The long term trends are built by fundamental factors that are founded on numerous economic pieces over a specific period of time.

For example, the currency pair GBP/USD has started an uptrend a year ago, and this trend continued ever since. On the other hand, EUR/GBP is following a falling trend for some time now.

Market Sentiment

By now, you already understand that trading in the forex market can be difficult especially for beginners. Market sentiment refers to the momentum of the market. All forex traders have their own style in trading - some may be bearish, and some may be bullish. Hence, market sentiment is the style of the different traders combined, which produces the general condition of the market.

There are instances that every indicator is pointing in a specific direction but the market is moving in the opposite. There are instances that the fundamental condition of the economy can be considered as bearish for a particular currency, and nevertheless, it keeps on fluctuating upwards in comparison with other currencies.

Price Action

Focusing on a single currency pair one at a time is a good way to be familiar with the general market sentiment. Through this, you can gradually master reading currency pairs.

Many lucrative forex traders are successfully trading according to their price action sense. In this strategy, you must keep track how quick a specific pair is moving in the two directions.

When the uptrend is quicker than the downtrend, it means that the market is more open to buy immediately, which indicate a more bullish general market sentiment. In addition, you can also monitor how a currency pair responds to financial news that is relevant for the currency pair. For instance, if the economy in the UK is good, the GBP/USD could bounce up according to the recovering economic data. This signifies a more bearish general market sentiment.

Research Skills

When trading in the forex market, you should not trade on an impulse. You must be confident with your strategy and you can do this through research. In the past, you can do a background check of the hottest currency pairs by reading books, newspapers, and other traditional forms of information sources.

With the advent of the World Wide Web, there are now countless sources of information that you can use for your research. However, not all of these sources are reliable and can guide you to become a successful forex trader. In choosing a source to consult, make certain that this covers the currency pairs to buy or if it is time to sell your currencies based on different factors such as technical and fundamental analysis.

There are also reliable newspapers and publications that you can read, which includes interpretation of global news and how the current events could affect the forex market. Forex trading involves revisiting past basic economics, because politics can also affect the behavior of forex players. Hence, it is crucial that you are updated with significant non-financial news from around the world.

In order to develop a solid foundation in forex trading, you must be updated with important technical and fundamental developments in the industry. Successful forex traders usually have a thirst for information as well as the drive to look for all relevant data, which could affect the trade. Many traders even maintain a monitoring platform to keep up with major news breakthrough that can have considerable impact not only in the forex market but also in the global financial scene.

Focus and Control

Focus is another important skill for forex traders, which can increase the more that you practice it. With the emergence of numerous online resources promising to guide you on forex trading, you should be able to develop how to identify and focus your lens on the actionable trends that could affect your trade.

There are forex traders that are only focusing on specific types of currency pairs so they can put all of their efforts in projecting the movement of the trade. By focusing on these currencies, traders can develop competitive advantage compared to traders who don't focus on their trades.

Meanwhile, a successful trader should also learn how to control their emotions and follow specific strategy or trading plan. This is crucial in handling risks in forex trades by taking profits at specific points or using stop losses. There are strategies in place that allow traders to lose a bit on bad trades but gain more revenues from ideal trades. Bad traders are usually affected by their emotions, which influence the strategic implementation of their trading plan.

Risk Management

Risk Management is a skill that you should master to safeguard your trading capital from losses. This must be integrated in your trading strategy as early as you can in your forex trading career.

Risk management covers strategies such as risk to reward, scaling trades, and stop losses. Mastering this skill will allow you to obtain higher profits and prevent losing money.

For instance, many successful traders don't risk more than 2 per cent of their fund in a single trade. This will safeguard your account from any significant downturn and will allow you to safely trade using leverage.

Psychology

Successful traders are not only adept in the mathematics behind the forex trading platform. They are also masters of understanding the psychology of people behind the trade. Aside from observing the possible behavior of market players, a forex trader should also overcome psychological aspects such as greed and fear.

In forex trading, you should learn how to follow the rules of the game without allowing your emotions to distract your game plan. It is not easy to become a successful forex trader, but if you work through your plan and master yourself, you can win the game through skills and discipline.

Chapter 3 - Top Strategies in Forex Trading

Aside from technical analysis and fundamental analysis, there are other strategies that are commonly used by forex traders today. This includes the following:

1. Carry Trade Trading
2. Pivot Trading
3. Position Trading
4. Reversal Trading
5. Retracement Trading
6. Breakout Trading
7. Swing Trading
8. Momentum Trading
9. Range Trading
10. Trend Trading

In this Chapter, we will discuss each trading strategy briefly, so you can choose the best strategy for you and later on expand your knowledge of these strategies.

Carry Trading

Carry Trading is a common forex trading strategy, which aims to increase profits through the differences in interest rates between two currencies. Usually, the currencies you buy and hold can pay for the interest rate between banks of the two currencies. In carry trading, you need to search a currency of a country with lower interest rate so you can purchase a currency by paying higher interest rate.

Forex traders could employ a strategy for trend trading in combination with carry trading to make sure that the price differences as well as the interest earned could complement each other and avoid offsetting their benefits.

Pivot Points Trading

In pivot trading, you need to identify the support and resistance levels according to the average of the past forex session's low and high closing rates. This average can help forex traders project the most likely lows and highs as well as market reversals in a matter of days.

Since averages are common in the forex market, these are regarded as a safe range for medium-term to long-term trading. These averages can also help a trader to determine if a new breakout is happening or a specific range is on the brim of being surpassed.

Position Trading

This forex trading strategy is ideal for traders who are looking for long-term gains, which could play out over several periods of months or even years. Traders who are into position trading usually base their plan on long-term trends of various economies. They also usually operate with minimal levels of leverage and smaller trade sizes with the projection of possibly gaining revenues on large price movements.

Position traders are often adept in using technical indicators as well as fundamental analysis in selecting their exit and entry levels. This form of trading may need higher levels of patience as well as stamina, and may not be ideal for those who are looking for quick profits.

Reversal Trading

Reversal trading refers to the form of trading that allow traders to look for a reversal in a price trend with the objective to guarantee entrance into any trade ahead of the market. This trading strategy is regarded as risky and not ideal for beginners. It can be difficult to spot true reversals, but these are also more rewarding if they are properly projected.

Traders are using different tools to identify reversals like volume indicators, momentum, or visual cues on charts like head-and-shoulder trends as well as triple tops and bottoms.

Retracement Trading

Retracement Trading is based on the concept that prices don't flow in perfect lines between lows and highs, and typically make some type of slow down and may even change their direction between strong resistance and support levels.

Forex traders will usually choose a certain portion of movement as an indicator of confirmation like 50 per cent or depend on Fibonacci ratio of 61.8 per cent, 38.2 per cent, or 23.6 per cent to help in identifying optimal points for exiting and entering trades.

Breakout Trading

In breakout trading, you need to determine a trade entry point in a specific breakout from a certain trading range in the prior range. When the price breaks in a higher range from a certain resistance level in a chart, you need to buy currency with the projection that it will persist its upward direction. Likewise, when the price breaks in a level of support inside a range, the trader can sell with the objective of buying the currency again at a more reasonable rate.

Swing Trading

This medium-term forex trading strategy is typically used over a period of days to weeks. Swing traders will usually look to set up trades on swings to lows and highs over a certain period of time. Its purpose is to filter out the erratic movements in the price, which is common in intraday trading. This is also used to prevent setting narrowly placed stop losses, which can force the traders to stop out a trade for a short-term market flow.

Momentum Trading

Momentum trading is based on the concept that strong price movements in a certain direction are possible indicators that there is a persistent price trend in a particular direction. Likewise, weakening movements signify that a trend has already lost its strength and can be headed towards a reversal. Momentum trading may also consider both volume and price, and usually use analysis of graphic tools such as candlestick charts and oscillators.

Range Trading

Range Trading is a basic strategy that is based on the concept that prices can typically hold inside a steady and predictable range for a specific period of time. This is specifically true in markets that involve steady and predictable economies as well as currencies that are often stable.

Forex traders who are into range trading depend on being able to regularly buy and sell at expected highs and lows of support and resistance, sometime doing several trades in a day. Range traders also use some of the same tools as trend traders to look for ideal exit and entry levels, which include the relative strength index as well as the stochastics and commodity channel index.

Trend Trading

Trend Trading is a popular forex trading strategy that involves spotting downwards or upwards trend in a price movement of a currency and selecting trade exits and entry points according to the position of the price currency inside the trend as well as the relative strength of the trend.

Take note that recent trends can be effective indicators of where rates are likely to go upward and where to best set up exits and entry points for the trade. Trend traders are also using different tools to assess the trends like stochastics, directional indices, volume measurements, relative strength indicators, and moving averages.

Chapter 4 - Tips & Tricks in Forex Trading

It is true that the forex market is filled with ratios, charts, and numbers. However, this game is more of an art than science. Similar to artistic endeavors, talent is a strong foundation, but it will only get you so far with your effort and improvement.

Successful traders develop their skills through discipline and practice. They perform self-evaluation to see what is driving their trades and learn how they can keep greed and fear out of the equation. In this Chapter, we will discuss the tips and tricks that a beginner can use to become successful in forex trading.

1. Establish your goals and select a trading style that is compatible for your personality

Before beginning a single trade in the forex market, it is crucial that you have some concept of where you want to go and how you can work every day to achieve this destination. Also, it is crucial that your goals in mind are clear as to what you want to achieve. You should also be certain that the trading strategy you choose will help you achieve your goals.

Take note that every type of trading strategy requires a specific approach and every style is suitable to different risk profiles. For instance, day trading can be ideal for you if you are not comfortable with an open position in the market. Meanwhile, if you have capital that you believe will take advantage from the appreciation of a trade over a period of several months, then position trading might be ideal for you. Just make certain that your personality is suitable for the trading style you do.

2. Select a trading methodology and be consistent

Before you start any trade, you should have enough knowledge about the forex market so you can execute your trades with confidence. You should know the specific information you need so you can make the best decision about whether to exit or enter a trade. Some traders are using technical analysis, while others prefer to look at the underlying fundamentals of the economy of the company, and then use charts to find out the best time to enter the trade.

Take note that market fundamentals can drive the long-term trend. Chart patterns, on the other hand, may provide you short-term trading opportunities. Just be consistent regardless of the methodology you prefer, and make certain to be flexible as well. The methodology must catch up with the changing forex market platform.

3. Carefully select your entry and exit frames

Most beginners in forex trading experience confusion because of the opposing data that they may encounter in evaluating charts in various time frames. For example, the information that can be extracted from an intraday chart could indicate a sell signal, which may show up as a buying signal when viewed in a weekly chart.

Hence, if you depend on an intraday chart and using a weekly chart to look for the best time entry, make certain that the two charts are in sync. When the weekly chart indicates a buying signal, you should also wait until the daily chart also shows a buying signal.

4. Work on the trade expectancy

It is crucial to make sure that whichever system you use, it should be reliable. You can do this by calculating on the expectancy. Using a formula, you can revisit past trends and gauge all the trades that you won against the trades that you lost. Then, you can figure out the profitability of the winning trades against how much you have lost on losing trades.

Checkout your previous 10 trades, then figure out if you have made profit or loss. Write the trades down and get the total of all the trades you won then divide the answer by the number of trades you lose. Below is the formula. W refers to the average winning trade, L refers to the average losing trade, while P refers to the percentage of winning ratio.

$$E = [1 + (W/L)] \times P - 1$$

For example, in your previous 10 trades, you have won seven trades, and three losses, 70 per cent is your win ratio. If the seven trades gained $3,000, then the average win is $3000/7 = $428.57. If your total loss were $ 1,000, then your average loss is $1,000/3 = $ 333.33.

In using the formula above, you will get: E=[1+ (428.57/333.33)] x 0.7 -1 = 0.60 or 60%, which means 60 per cent reliability of the system that can provide you 60 cents on a dollar in the long run.

5. Create positive feedback loops

You can create a positive feedback loop if your trades are implemented according to your strategic plan. A positive feedback pattern can be created if you execute a trade based on your plan. Success can breed success, which could in turn provide the confidence you need, especially if the trade is profitable. The habit of sticking to your plan, despite of some losses that you may encounter in the process can still result to positive feedback loop.

6. Concentrate on your trading strategy and don't be afraid of small losses

In playing the forex market, you should take note that there is a risk to lose all your money. Hence, you should only use your excess money and not gamble your money for necessities such as college fund. Successful traders consider their trading fund as a game fund. When the game is over, the money is all spent.

This attitude can help you to be more positive while trading in the forex. Psychologically, you can be well-prepared to accept even small losses. This is crucial in how you can handle risks successfully. You can become a successful forex trader if you concentrate on your trades and learn from small losses.

Chapter 5 - Common Forex Trading Mistakes to Avoid

While you can make substantial gains from forex trading in a single day, there is also the risk of losing all of your money in a single trade. This is especially true if you don't know how to use leverage for your advantage or commit specific practices that if you use could end up draining your fund.

There are common forex trading mistakes that forex traders usually make in the hope to gain high returns, but end up losing a lot of money. With knowledge, discipline, and alternative methodologies, you can avoid these trading mistakes.

Averaging Down

Beginners in the Forex market usually experience difficulty when it comes to averaging down. Most of these traders commit this mistake unintentionally. The primary concern with averaging down is not only it can cost you money but also time, which could be allocated on other trades that can provide you better returns.

Meanwhile, a higher return is required on remaining fund in order to initiate replenishment. If you lose half of your capital, it will require 100% return in order to gain back your capital to its original level. Losing huge chunks of capital on a single day or on a single trade can easily cripple down the growth of your capital in time.

While averaging down may work on special circumstances, this strategy will eventually result to margin call or substantial loss, because a trend can only sustain itself depending on the liquidity of the trader.

News Prepositioning

While you may be aware of certain news events that can influence the market, the direction is still uncertain. You might even be confident on the possible news such as the movement of interest rates in a country, but there is no way to accurately project how the exchange will behave after the news. There are also added news or indicators behind the news announcements, which could make the movement highly illogical yet possible.

All sort of orders can also hit the market and stops could be triggered on different sides of the currency pair. This usually lead to a back and forth action prior to an emergence of a trend. Taking a position prior to a news announcement can substantially damage your probability of winning the trade.

Quick Trading after News Announcement

A news announcement hits the market and then the market players will start to react. At first, it seems like no-brainer to ride the bandwagon so you can take advantage of the market sentiment. If you do this without a plan and without formidable trading strategy, you may end up losing the trade.

News releases usually result to fluctuation in the market mainly because of hair-pin turns and lack of liquidity in the market assessment of the report. There are even trades that are already in the money end up quickly turning and bringing large losses as significant swings happen around. Liquidity is crucial for these times, which could mean that losses can probably be much more than expected.

Successful traders usually wait for some time so the volatility could subside so there will be a definitive trend after the hype.

Trading More than 1% of Your Capital in a Single Trade

Take note that higher returns doesn't always mean higher risk. Most traders who risk huge amounts of money on a single trade will typically lose in the long term. A common rule of the thumb is that you should only risk not higher than 1 per cent of the capital on one trade. If you have accumulated enough experience and skills in forex trading, you can increase your limit to 2 per cent.

You must also establish a daily maximum risk, which can be for beginners 1 % of the capital or equal to the average daily profit in a month. For instance, if you have $100,000 in your account (without the leverage), you should not lose $1,000 in a single day.

With this strategy, you can make certain that no single day of trading or single trade could affect the account substantially.

Unrealistic Projections

Regardless of your dreams or goals in forex trading, the market is insensitive to what you expect. Before you even start trading, you should accept the fact that the forex market could be illogical and volatile.

In order to avoid disappointments from unrealistic expectations, you should have a trading plan and stick to this strategy when you are doing the actual trade. If the results are steady, still stick to your trade plane. In the forex market, even a minor gain could become substantial in the long run.

As your fund grows over time, the position size could be increased so you can bring in higher returns. Also, if you want to test a new strategy, you should only do so with minimal capital. You can allocate more capital into a strategy if you see positive results.

The forex market is also quite volatile near the open. You can use certain strategies in the opening, which are not ideal near the closing. The market may become more stable as the day progresses and there may be a pickup in action towards the close that may require another form of strategy. The key in this fluctuating market is to accept what is provided by the market and don't expect too much from the system.

CONCLUSION

Thank you again for purchasing this book!

I hope this book was able to help you gain a basic understanding of forex trading and start earning money every day.

The next step is to open your account and face the challenge of winning forex trades.

Finally, if you enjoyed this book, then I'd like to ask you for a favor, would you be kind enough to leave a review for this book on Amazon? It'd be greatly appreciated!

Thank you and good luck!

Preview Of 'Penny Stocks'

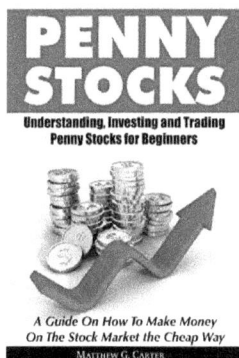

This book has actionable information on how to invest in penny stocks, trade penny stocks and make money in the process.

Investing in stocks is undoubtedly one of the best investment vehicles the world over. And it is not just the high value stocks that cost tens, hundreds or even thousands of dollars per share; even if you invest in stocks that cost less than $10 or even less than $5 per share, you stand a good chance to make a lot of money in the process, especially in capital gains. If you cannot afford to spare 10s, 100s or even 1000s of dollars per share, perhaps penny stocks are the way to go. Even if you are completely new to stocks trading and penny stocks in particular, you can learn everything there is to learn about these and succeed at it. There is just so much money to be made trading in penny stocks and this book will show you exactly what you need to do.

If you are one of those people who think that you have to be a trading prodigy to invest in penny stocks then you are very wrong. Penny stocks, just like any other stocks and securities, require you to be well informed, disciplined and have good strategies while participating in order to succeed- and this is what this guide is meant for. It will give you sufficient knowledge that you will require to get started as a penny stock trader inclusive of how to trade, calculating your profits, avoiding penny stocks hazards and much more!

Penny Stock: What Is It?

In simple terms, a penny stock is basically a low priced stock that is trading under $5. They are common stocks owned and made available by small public companies. The low price of penny stock shares allows an investor to hold many shares (typically thousands) at the same time for a small amount of invested capital. This explains why penny stocks are so appealing and offer competitive advantage to small and medium sized investors.

Most people make money off penny stocks by benefiting from the capital gains i.e. the appreciation of price of shares, as most penny stocks don't pay dividends.

As amazing as this sounds, this profit model makes penny stocks also highly risky- as much as they offer high returns. This is because of one major reason- they are more prone to scams.

Check out the rest of *'Penny Stocks: Understanding, Investing and Trading Penny Stocks for Beginners A Guide On How To Make Money On The Stock Market the Cheap Way'* on Amazon.

www.ingramcontent.com/pod-product-compliance
Lightning Source LLC
Chambersburg PA
CBHW071115210326
41519CB00020B/6306